Through this book, Tanya shares her most intimate thoughts and feelings—courageously exposing her true self to the world. Her collection of stories and poems is pure, authentic and powerful. Bravo!

—Natacha Belair, Author of *A Stellar Purpose*

Your book gave me hope. It reminded me of the strength I have within and the trust that I continue to hold. This book is a support for resilience no matter what you are moving through in life—we are all moving through it together.

—Ashley Hämäläinen, Cofounder of *A Line Within* and host of *A Line Podcast*

To be present in these pages is to experience what it means to let go and know that you are being held by something so much bigger than yourself. It is to stand tall in your truth and to know that the quiet whisper deep within is always on your side. It is to be brave, to be honest, to be gentle.

—Genevieve G. Georget, Developmental editor and founder of *Gray & Granite Magazine*

I wish you to take moments of silence and presence, guided by the power of the words transmitted by Tanya, to give yourself the gift of listening to what your essence is trying to transmit to you, through your own transformative life experiences.

—Marie-Pierre Chaumont, Spiritual teacher, speaker and author

Solstice

There is no greater agony than bearing an untold story inside of you.

—*Maya Angelou*

To the homebody, keep this book on your bedside table.
To the nomad, keep this book in your travel bag.

Keep this book close to your heart to bring you comfort in challenging times of incertitude or moments of quietude.

This creation will burst your heart open, manifesting space for contemplation and understanding of the majestic, glorious, and spectacular being you are.

It will embrace you gently throughout your metamorphosis, so you know that you are not alone.

We are all in this together.
We always need to be there for each other.

Solstice

noun: solstice; plural noun: solstices
The time or date (twice each year) at which the sun reaches its maximum or minimum declination, marked by the longest and shortest days (about June 21 and December 22)

Table of Contents

Dedication	13
Foreword	17
God	29
Author's Note	33
Déjà Vu	39
Speaking My Truth	53
The Cardinals	61
Soul-Searching	67
Healing	133
Emerging	249
The Last Mile	271
Butterfly Tattoo	289
Thank You	295
The Author	305

Dedication

To my husband, Stéphane. Thank you for being my rock, being fully present, and loving me unconditionally in all the wonderful and more difficult times. I am a better human being because of you. I love you and we are soulmates, forever and always.

To my son Jacob and my daughter Maïka. When life brings you challenges, know that you have everything already within you to go through those challenges and withstand them with strength and grace. Trust yourself entirely and know that you are always guided, supported, and deeply loved. I am truly blessed that both of your souls chose me to be your mother.

Solstice is also dedicated to all my family, friends, colleagues, doctors, healers, and the inspiring cancer survivors I had the honor of meeting and sharing my journey with. I am grateful for you. I love you, and you know who you are.

To all humans on a quest for healing, transformation, and inspiration. It is by healing ourselves that we encourage others to do the same, creating a rippling effect for a new and improved world to blossom for the generations to come.

Foreword

ASHLEY HÄMÄLÄINEN

Cofounder of *A Line Within* and host of *A Line Podcast*

I remember the day vividly. I was standing in my office feeling called to message Tanya back. We had been communicating about work projects and how she was going to take some time off to focus on taking care of herself and wasn't sure she'd be able to create for a while. I remember thinking, *But that is your medicine and you cannot stop creating. Whether you're doing so for someone else or for yourself, you must create as often as you can throughout this healing process—do not stop creating.* I remember sending the message and wondering if I had overstepped my boundaries. Had I said too much? After reading this book, I know with certainty, no—I did not say too much.

Tanya, this book is pure medicine. I read it with tears in my eyes the entire time because, although I am not going through cancer at the moment, I am moving through the most transformational journey of my whole life. One year ago, I had a house, things, land, and stability. Suddenly, I received a message from God to let it all go and return back to love.

In doing so, I have found my soulmate, and we've gotten married. I am pregnant.

However, we are still on a journey to find our home, living in Airbnbs and surrendering to guidance along the way, and it has been so, so challenging for me. Your book gave me hope. It reminded me of the strength I have within and the trust that I continue to hold. This book is a support for resilience no matter what you are moving through in life—we are all moving through it together.

GENEVIEVE G. GEORGET
Developmental editor and founder of *Gray & Granite Magazine*

When I was a little girl, my grandmother lived with us for a while. She slept in the spare bedroom at the front of the house. She wore an oversized nightgown, read books with a giant magnifying glass, and ate chocolate chip cookies for most meals of the day. She was one of my most favorite humans in the entire world—filled with gentleness and patience and just the right amount of troublemaker!

I was eleven years old when she caught pneumonia one winter and ended up in the intensive care unit.

I remember sitting in a brightly lit hallway across from a nurse's station. The chairs were a light green faux leather, and there was a red "NO ENTRY BEYOND THIS POINT" sign on the two giant doors that stood beside me. I knew that my grandmother was on the other side of those doors.

My small fingers played with a loose string that hung from beneath the chair, and my legs swung as people moved around me.

Time moves differently when you're young. Eventually, the automatic doors swung open, and my mother walked through with a nurse by her side.

My mother reached out her hand toward me, and as I looked over at the nurse, dressed in light blue scrubs, she smiled kindly and nodded her head.

"It's OK," the nurse quietly said.

The dim lighting in the ICU was a stark contrast to the bright overheads that filled every corner of the hallways, and I remember the sounds of machines humming and people crying and nurses whispering. There were six beds in this specific unit, and my grandmother lay still at the very end, right next to the window.

My mother ushered me over to the left side of her bed, her hand resting on my shoulder.

I don't know how long it took before the panic set in, but I remember the overwhelming feeling of it all.

The smell.
The sound.
The sight.

This wasn't my grandmother. It couldn't be.

My grandmother played cards and drove a motorized scooter to breakfast and always had a cat sleeping on her lap. This woman had tubes coming out of her mouth and an ugly green robe and a look of deep sadness in her eyes that I had never seen before.

I was quickly taken out of the ICU and placed back in the same chair across from the nurse's station.

My grandmother died a couple of days later, and my breathing has never remained steady in a hospital or doctor's office ever since.

I grew up to become an adult with an above-average fear of illness. Witnessing how disease strips us of life became a memory that my mind was never able to shake. Combined with other circumstances that happened along the way, I learned to distrust my body—to feel unsafe in the one home that I was given to live out this life.

If my grandmother's body could turn on her the way that it did, it felt like too big of a risk to consider my own a friend.

I'll admit that I had to sit with the request a little bit before agreeing to step in as developmental editor for this book. Tanya's message came as I was in the throes of an intense season of anxiety around my own health, and I wasn't entirely sure if I could remain grounded enough to support the story in the manner with which it deserved to be honored.

But something about Tanya's words and sense of calm drew me toward the project in a way that I knew was about more than poetry.

It was about healing.
It was about transformation.
It was about using art to metabolize what it means to be human.

And so, I dove into Tanya's gorgeous body of work, both as an editor and as a first reader. I allowed myself to be embraced by her story and gently moved by her journey. And in turn, I was faced with a pivotal question: could my body actually be my ally, my friend, my cocreator on this path we all walk through the mountains of life?

I don't consider it a coincidence that a manuscript on the transformative power of disease landed in my lap at the very time that I was struggling to listen to my own internal voice.

I needed a shift in perspective.
I needed a narrative with which to build a new foundation.
I needed a gentle hand to show me what was possible.
This book is all of that.

To be present in these pages is to experience what it means to let go and know that you are being held by something so much bigger than yourself. It is to stand tall in your truth and to know that the quiet whisper deep within is always on your side. It is to be brave, to be honest, to be gentle . . .

It is to be love.

MARIE-PIERRE CHAUMONT
Spiritual teacher, speaker and author

At the age of 24, I was diagnosed with stage 3 Hodgkins cancer.

Before this shattering experience, I had never danced with the disease. I was living a life already mapped out: I had gotten married less than a year earlier, my communications career was booming, and we were about to start a family.

On paper, my life looked perfect.

But without knowing it, I was completely uprooted from my essence. I had never taken a moment to ask myself who I was, but above all, who I wanted to be. I was on autopilot and spent my days completely uprooted from my body, already numbed by the human experience.

Through cancer, chemotherapy treatments and times when I felt buried under my fears and doubts, I promised myself that I would never return to this life that had made me sick.

But, despite my good intentions, I had not quite absorbed the multiple gift lessons imparted by this transformative experience. Without realizing it, I gradually returned to my old life and I forgot these beautiful promises I had made to myself.

But the Universe had not forgotten them (and he has a long memory!). He gave me a few years of respite but, seeing that I had no intention of changing paths, he sent me a second teacher, even more powerful than cancer, in the form of a burnout spectacular.

Ouch.

This forced stoppage of 6 months, during which I no longer even had the energy to take care of my children, to take a shower, to get up from my sofa, brought the reality of my experience back to my face. human, but above all, of my propensity to flee my emotions and to repress my feelings. At 30, I was once again deeply uprooted from my essence and this time, I could no longer run away from these realizations that were knocking insistently at my door.

So I listened, for real.

Over my months, to help me with the exhaustion and anxiety I was experiencing, I discovered the power of silence and meditation. I became aware of the magnificent presence of the Universe which guides and supports me. I realized that I carried within me an ability to connect with the Guides and to transmit their messages (for a girl from Abitibi who had never heard of the Guides, it was quite a surprise!).

But above all, I saw with clarity that, despite the promise I had made to myself following cancer, I had not honored my desire to live a life that allowed me to be. And over the months, I began to make conscious decisions to honor my sacred promise to live a simpler, smoother, more aligned life.

Gradually, I gave myself permission not to follow this pre-established path and instead forged my own path as a spiritual teacher.

Just as Tanya's book teaches us so well, it's never too late to listen to yourself and to honor yourself, with love and compassion. Succeeding in life isn't about living the perfect life, having all the answers, and never being wrong. God knows I am very human and will continue to take a multitude of detours in my path, especially when I am not listening to the needs of my body and soul.

But all these stormy (and above all precious!) life experiences that I have lived inspire me every day to make the conscious choice to stop from time to time, to look at myself with clarity, to validate if I am alignment. And if not, if I have fallen into the vortex and lost my integrity of Being, I simply choose to slow down, to better come back into my presence, guided by my quest for a life cheerful and aligned. This is what I wish for you, as you read this magnificent book.

I wish you to take moments of silence and presence, guided by the power of the words transmitted by Tanya, to give yourself the gift of listening to what your essence is trying to transmit to you, through your own transformative life experiences.

And for you, Tanya: bravo for your courage. Not only in the face of cancer, but especially for your ability to welcome your vulnerability and your journey towards healing, with love and compassion. Thank you for your wonderful work of light.

xo, Marie Pierre

God

The word God has been used sparingly in my book for a very purposeful reason. God, goddess, source, universe, higher self, or life-force energy, all of these names are valuable and beautiful to represent this unconditional force of love that creates life. I believe we are all interconnected and a special and unique part of this almighty, compassionate, and loving force.

In my heart, God is a pure and unlimited loving energy flowing through every single thing. It also has no gender. God is this abundant, limitless, and magnificent ocean that each of us, as one single drop, is a part of. We are all a divine and perfect spark of God, and our souls choose to come here on Earth school to volunteer, grow, evolve, and share our gifts to help others. When we truly realize it, our perspective and outlook on life changes tremendously, and we start to experience more gratitude, compassion, and love toward ourselves, others, and every living thing around us. This book is for YOU. I want you to feel free and be entirely at ease replacing the word God for any other word that represents to YOU the ultimate source of love that we are all created from.

Author's Note

Sitting at my favorite cozy neighborhood cafe, the rain pouring against the window, I feel nervous and peaceful at the same time. Today, June 21, 2022, is my birthday. As I write these words, it's the summer solstice and my forty-fourth turn around the sun.

I've always felt immensely blessed that my soul decided to make her grand entrance on earth on this very special day. The beginning of a season, a brand-new cycle, and the longest day of the year. Also, a very potent energy portal, opening up new opportunities for growth and transformation.

In March of this year, I was diagnosed with thyroid cancer. It has been raw, intense, and chaotic but a significant and transformative experience as well. In the midst of my anger, my sadness, and all of my fears, as a creative soul, I was drawn to write my feelings and inspirations down. Never would I have known that my first book would be born.

Solstice is a compilation of my own channeled intimate reflections, nuggets of wisdom, and poems I've written throughout this larger-than-life journey and has been a wonderful outlet for me to truthfully welcome the possibility to connect inward and fully embody this absolute love and compassion for myself.

Writing this book also helped me find solace, peace, and bliss in this chaotic season of my life, and I am very grateful for it. The journey is not over.

Healing is not linear and has many bumps along the road. It is our life's work. I trust with certainty that this experience will be one of the most significant lessons, redirecting me on the right path for my highest good and growth. One day at a time, I am learning to shed whatever is no longer in alignment with my soul and to choose love and joy instead.

I hope *Solstice* will bring you comfort and support in your own beautiful, messy, and remarkable metamorphosis. Know that you are always loved and supported no matter what you are going through. Never underestimate the warrior you are. We each have a fire within us waiting to be lit. You are fierce and powerful beyond measure, and love will always be the greatest medicine you will find.

I see you. I hear you. I love you. Unconditionally.

Tanya xx

Like the caterpillar
emerging into a
beautiful butterfly,
I am renewed in
a way I could never
have imagined.

Déjà Vu

I clearly remember feeling under the weather as a young teenager, sitting down at my neighborhood's walk-in clinic with my mother, seeking help from a physician to soothe the torturing soreness I'd been feeling in my throat for many days. Having a weak immune system, I was frequently susceptible to experiencing strep throat infections, which required antibiotics many times a year to kill the viruses I was constantly battling, mostly in wintertime.

I explicitly recall the light and uninviting painted walls that adorned the waiting room, the harsh smell of disinfectant irritating my lungs, and the large round table full of old fashion magazines containing multiple missing pages from the most intriguing articles I wanted to read. Eerie was the feeling the room was issuing: always crowded with people patiently waiting next to each other with no chairs available for sitting. Sniffling, coughing, and complaining were the most common sounds you could hear in between the walls.

After waiting for some time, I was called to come in. After explaining all the familiar symptoms I'd been experiencing, I was only expecting to be prescribed an antibiotic and return home relieved that it would all pass. Drinking plenty of water, sipping warm homemade soup, and resting was my best medicine. The general doctor who was on shift that afternoon checked my throat, took a little swab to send to the lab, and told me I would get a call soon with the results. I was ready to leave the office but before I had the chance to get out, the practitioner stopped me briskly and asked me to come back. He then directed me to turn around and show him my back. "Could you please bend over for me so I can check your spine?" he asked.

After a few minutes, while analyzing my posture and evaluating my spine, he discovered something that would change the course of my life forever.

"Tanya, you have a severe case of scoliosis," he began to share. "It is a sideways curvature of the spine that is most often diagnosed in adolescents. No one knows what the root cause of this disability is. You will need surgery as soon as possible at the children's hospital in Montréal, Canada. If you don't get it, your spine could perforate your organs, and you could die. You also may not be able to bear children since this would be too dangerous for your health and the baby."

Leaving the office, paralyzed with fear of the unknown, the idea I had of the perfect world was shattered in a matter of seconds. Powerless and scared, I walked to the car with my mother, who was also in shock and denial. We sat down, closed the doors, and started weeping endlessly together, not knowing what would come next after hearing this very upsetting announcement.

How could I live a normal teenage girl life knowing this crippling impairment was now a part of me? Would boys be disgusted or frightened to date me? Would I be able to have children one day? Would I be suffering indefinitely or have any sense of a normal life? It was a moment that has since been engraved in my mind.

Weeks after the diagnosis, my parents and I decided to get a second opinion from a specialist at our local children's hospital. Fast forward after a lot of poking, X-rays, and scans, I was advised not to undergo surgery. It was definitely a relief, but I knew I had to accept living with this disability for the rest of my life.

I had to make peace with my new condition and learn to manage the discomfort and restrictions that came along with it. My scoliosis has consistently been uncomfortable, painful, and restrictive, but I've never let it define who I am. Today, I am alive. I am married to the love of my life and have two beautiful and healthy children.

Decades after the scoliosis, severe digestive problems, a feeling as though I had a lump in my throat, and extreme fatigue started to occur regularly. Sometimes the pain was so unbearable that I couldn't get out of bed in the morning, eat, work, or get a good night's sleep. After multiple blood tests, lengthy visits to the emergency room, ultrasounds, scans, and an endoscopy, the results always came back negative. Intuitively, I was guided to dig deeper and not take these results as the final outcome.

Even after drastically changing my diet, reading countless books, and listening to a galore of podcasts on the subject, I was still aching on a regular basis. A wildfire was constantly burning fiercely in my stomach area that no amount of water could extinguish. Just thinking of food was triggering for me. My body was completely exhausted.

Most of my morning routine consisted of staying in bed in a seated position to reduce the nausea. I was losing more and more weight and had entirely lost my appetite for food and life in general. It was an interminable cycle that needed to end once and for all.

On another dreadful morning, waking up again with the mass lodged in my throat and feeling worse than ever, I finally chose to trust my instinct and scheduled another appointment with my compassionate family physician who was continuingly supporting me on my healing journey. I mentioned that my intuition guided me to ask for one last ultrasound of my neck and throat, and to go from there. She agreed.

With saddened validation, the scan revealed some abnormal thyroid nodules and enlarged lymph nodes in my neck. I was then scheduled to have a fine needle aspiration biopsy, a procedure where a small sample of tissue from the thyroid gland and lymph nodes is removed and sent to a lab for analysis.

On Tuesday, March 22, 2022, lying on a freezing cold metal table in the early afternoon, I was so nervous about the unknown, and my heart was pounding out of my chest like a clock. One very friendly nurse, a doctor, and a pathologist were present in the room. Seeing the longest needle I'd ever seen before being removed from its plastic bag was enough for me to feel dizzy.

Closing my eyes and taking long deep inhales and exhales calmed me down. I had to trust the medical professionals around me and surrender to whatever was going to happen. After an hour of being poked from left to right, it was finally over, and I was released to go home and get some well-deserved rest.

Friday of the same week, with all my family being diagnosed with Covid, including myself, was the day my world got turned upside down. It was late in the afternoon. I was in the kitchen preparing dinner. My husband was working on his laptop in the den and our kids were in their bedrooms when suddenly, my phone rang. I instantly knew it was the ear and throat specialist who was calling with the biopsy results.

"Tanya, are you sitting down? I have your biopsy report. You have papillary thyroid cancer," the doctor told me on a five-minute phone call. "It is a good cancer, but you will need surgery to remove your entire thyroid gland and all the affected lymph nodes. You will also need radioactive iodine treatments afterward. It will not be easy, but it is highly treatable."

The thyroid gland is a butterfly-shaped organ located in the base of the neck and is part of the endocrine system. It releases hormones called triiodothyronine (T3) and thyroxine (T4) that control a person's metabolism—the way a body uses energy. The thyroid's hormones regulate vital body functions, including breathing, heart rate, central and peripheral nervous systems, body weight, muscle strength, menstrual cycles, body temperature, cholesterol levels, and much more. It is an essential organ in your body. If the gland is removed, specific medication will be required for the rest of the person's lifetime.

It was déjà vu . . .

Strangely similar to that unforgettable day at the overly sterilized and eerie walk-in clinic where I received my scoliosis diagnosis.

After hanging up the phone, my body couldn't move. It felt like I was paralyzed from head to toe. Time stood still. I sat for a while on our living room sofa, suffocating and breathless. My brain shattered into millions of pieces and was unable to process the information I'd just received. My only reaction was to walk straight into the den where my husband was sitting and share with him that I had cancer. Vocalizing this specific word from my mouth for the first time was excruciating, destabilizing, and unreal. Before he had the chance to voice anything, I fell on my knees in front of him and started bawling. Tears were flowing endlessly. Desperate and scared, I had to let them all out in hopes of feeling some relief. Later on, I called my parents to share the upsetting news with them. Being a parent myself, I can't even imagine how torturous it must have been for them to receive a call like this one.

What will the next step be?
Will I be in constant pain?
Will I need chemotherapy in addition to radiation?
Will I lose my hair?
Will I be able to function normally during the months ahead?
What will the kids say?
How will they react and deal with this?
Will I have to take a leave of absence from work?

Suddenly, my life was interrupted.

I was undoubtedly not prepared to confront this. The first few weeks were very emotionally intense. Disbelief, unshakable sadness, unsettling anxiety, desperation, and disgust continually flooded my entire body and mind. I was now a new person and was already grieving the woman I was before. I cried until I had no tears left to cry. I felt angry with myself for being clueless about the disease making its home and multiplying within my physical body, probably for many years and certainly without any invitation.

I knew I had a very important decision to make that would change the entire course of my healing journey. I could either wake up and go to bed engulfed with fear and anxiety or make a conscious choice to remain present and be open to the experience with an open heart and infinite love and compassion. I knew I still had to continue on and have stability around me for my husband and kids. I also knew that making the intention to remain in the highest vibration possible would also help me sail the waters with more ease and increase my chance of recovery.

Little did I know at the time that these health trials would later become a miracle. With a new perspective, I now realize that if the digestive upsets I'd been having over these past few years had never occurred and if I hadn't followed my internal compass—demanding to get a last ultrasound—the cancer would have probably been found at a later time in a more advanced stage.

On July 25, exactly four months after my diagnosis, the waiting game was over. I was admitted to the hospital at the crack of dawn. I was asked to change out of my comfy clothes and into a typical unflattering hospital gown while I waited on a stretcher for a nurse to come and prepare me for the surgery. Nervous, frightened, and shivering from the cold, I listened as the anesthesiologist explained every step of the operation to me in detail. A while later, all alone and waiting in the empty hall a few feet from the operating room, I remember closing my eyes and grounding my body to the Earth for peace and protection. I prayed and asked that all hands that would be in contact with me during and after the surgery be an extension of God's hands and that the procedure would go through effortlessly and perfectly.

I was fully aware that God, my team of invisible guides, angels, and ancestors were surrounding me in that instant. I also knew that all of my family and friends were thinking of me, and it was enough to give me the courage I needed to go through it.

I was lying down, unconscious for a total of five hours. My surgeon carefully and meticulously removed my entire thyroid gland and eighteen cancerous lymph nodes located within my neck area. I found out afterward that the cancer was already at an advanced stage, and I was fortunate that it was caught before it spread any further. It was a complex but profound experience. I remained in the hospital for four days, sharing a room with another cancer patient. I was connected to two long tubes inserted in my neck, draining the excess fluid. I was also on heavy medication and unable to properly move or speak for many weeks. It was quite the ride, but when I returned home, I could begin to breathe a little easier.

As of today, on October 26, I am two weeks away from receiving my radioactive iodine treatment. I will have to stick to a specific low-iodine diet for the next few weeks, and I will be taking a small pill that will destroy the remaining parts of my thyroid gland and cancerous cells if any are left. Loss of taste, dry or watery eyes, inflammation of the salivary glands, and dry mouth are the most common side effects from the treatment.

As before the surgery, I surrender all my fears to God, and I know I will be carefully and lovingly held by the wings of the angels. This will hopefully be the last scary medical procedure I will have to endure as a result of this diagnosis. A week after the treatment, one last scan will be performed, revealing if the cancer has been completely removed. It also brings me peace of mind knowing that for the next ten years, an endocrinologist will be keeping an eye on me, making certain that the disease stays permanently dormant. I am now wearing two long scars, one at the base of my neck and one on my left side. Like a tattoo, I will be wearing them proudly forever. They remind me, every second, that I am stronger than the cancer that tried to hurt me and bring me down.

We will each encounter individual hardships and traumas that will surface during distinct phases of our existence. Suffering is inevitable and always leaves scars, be it physically, mentally, emotionally, or sometimes spiritually. We have to trust that the hardships and traumas are not happening to us but for us, showing up when we desperately need a change of course and leading us to something better and healthier. As our greatest teachers, they are coaching us to become more compassionate and more loving with ourselves and others. They are a reflection of our might and bravery.

Our duty is to acknowledge them, process them, and let them go with utmost compassion, acceptance, and love. When we let go of all the hefty baggage, we are creating more space for flow and ease. It is not always easy, but by surrounding ourselves with the love and support of other people, there is always a glimpse of hope available to all.

Reflecting on my past, I now comprehend that sometimes we will face specific challenges and traumas in our childhood that prepare us to handle more profound difficulties later on in our adulthood. The scoliosis, similar to the cancer, was here to teach my body, mind, and soul many valuable lessons I may not have learned if they wouldn't have manifested in my life. I am also grateful for all the recurring digestive problems I'd been dealing with. As brutal as they had been, they were the universe's way of leading me to trust my gut feelings and advocate for my own health so this slow and quiet disease could be discovered and treated before it was too late.

We may never fully understand why all the obstacles we face are sent our way. I, unfortunately, can't predict if the cancer will be in complete remission or come back someday. But what is in my control is continuing to focus on love, practicing daily self-care, and respecting my limits. This will at least increase my chances for optimal health.

Like the caterpillar developing into a beautiful butterfly, I am renewed in a way I could never have imagined. It has been such a precious season for me to pause, heal, restore, and recharge. A powerful test of trust, patience, faith, and strength—the making of a powerful transformation.

Open your
Vishuddha,
and you will
find your voice
and be free to
speak your truth.

Speaking My Truth

Earlier this year, discovering I was afflicted with thyroid cancer located within my throat chakra—the energy center responsible for communication, self-expression, and the ability to speak our personal truth—was truly an eye opener for me. It was now an opportunity to dig deeper into my unconscious to hopefully discover what may have played a role in developing sickness at this specific location of my body.

The chakras are the seven spiraling energy wheels in the body, starting from the crown of the head and down the body to the base of the spine. When all energy centers are spinning properly, they each allow energy to flow and move freely, meaning we are in harmony and alignment. However, if one of these wheels becomes blocked or out of alignment with the others, our well-being can suffer, disease can be created, and we can feel physically, mentally, or emotionally unbalanced.

The throat chakra, commonly known as Vishuddha in Sanskrit, is the energy center located in throat center. When there is a blockage within this region, it is often associated with the inability to speak, like something needs to be said but is difficult or impossible to let out, and a feeling as though there is a lump in the throat or a catch in the voice. This imbalance may also manifest as a fear of speaking in public or even talking openly with people we know. It is also associated with being silenced for a prolonged period of time or not practicing speaking our truth whenever it is for us.

Sometimes our truth may only be acknowledging what is not aligned with us anymore. We are constantly changing and evolving. As human beings, change is inevitable. It is a natural and organic process, allowing us to evolve and grow into our highest selves. At some point, our path may require some adjustments and a change of direction. We may even have to let go of certain parts of our lives that we've outgrown or that are not bringing us into a state of joy anymore, whether it is an occupation, a marriage, a friendship, or a home we lived in for many years and created many meaningful memories in.

But we have to be courageous and not let our fears, and the fears of others, fog our willingness to make that first step. Fear of judgment, fear of not being enough, fear of losing someone or something, or worrying about the unknown and what the future may be like if we choose to invite change to take place. Fear is an innate part of us. It has been thoughtfully designed and built within to protect us, so we remain in our cozy little comfort zone, keeping us safe. Unfortunately, it also strives to keep us small, stagnant, and further away from who we should become. Being continuously mindful of how much space we allow fear to hold in our everyday decisions can have a major impact in our life. We then, can create a more peaceful and healthier relationship with it.

In hindsight, it was crystal clear. I needed to let go of some heaviness and resistance I had been carrying for too long. First and foremost, I had to acknowledge them and all the uncomfortable imprinted emotions that were affecting me negatively and allow them to release gently, with utmost love and compassion. It was such hard inner work, and it still is. It will be a lifelong commitment but a precious gift and blessing.

Being present, mindful, and aware of my triggers allowed me to forge a new avenue within, leading me closer to my true self and to a powerful awakening.

Facing my demons, eye to eye, has been such a hard core, raw, and destabilizing experience. It felt heart-wrenching, intense, arduous, laborious, and grueling, ripping every familiar and homelike landmark I've been holding onto for most of my life.

I asked the air to blow away everything that was not serving me anymore. I commanded the roaring force of fire to extinguish my fears and reclaim my inner peace. I allowed the pureness of water to cleanse my body, mind, heart, and soul. I welcomed the grounding energy of Mother Earth to envelop and heal me to become whole again.

I needed to release self-judgment. I needed to release my fear of not pleasing others, agreeing to everyone's expectations, putting my own needs aside, and saying goodbye to many heavy emotions I was consciously or unconsciously hoarding inside me. Speaking my truth meant letting go of the fear of hurting the people around me, and doing so was profoundly liberating.

Also, I realized that for most of my professional career, working in a high-level security environment had built an invisible wall—shutting out my artistic voice that wanted so deeply to be shared—and also played an important role in me feeling trapped and choked, disabling my ability to fully embody who I was as an artist for many years. This, too, was a truly eye-opening immersion.

I am now called to make some decisions that will impact the next chapter of my life. I am fully aware I may have to grieve some fragments of the person I was before, some people and places I've acquainted with for a short period or a lifetime, and say farewell to many weakening habits that were draining my well and depleting my own self-worth and vital energy.

Cancer has most definitively placed a full body mirror in front of me, reflecting my own deeply rooted fears and giving me the space to confront them with love and compassion. It feels like the removal of my little butterfly-shaped gland and losing both of its wings has opened a portal of understanding for the growth of my spirit. I am already feeling my new wings growing, expanding, and I am being reborn again.

Where will my soul lead me without all these pesky resistances and fears lingering around anymore? I now know that everything is possible when we decide to let go of fear and contemplate the world through the lens of love.

From the day I received my cancer diagnosis and throughout my recovery process, this book has been my dearest and loyal companion—a safe and peaceful sanctuary that allowed powerful healing, maturation, and expansion to manifest within me. It escorted me gently through discovering my voice and fully expressing it with truthfulness and vulnerability. It is most definitely one of the most precious blessings I've ever been gifted with in my lifetime.

We each have our own personal and perfectly divine story inside of us that is worthy of being told. Sharing it with the purpose of spreading more beauty, healing, and a sense of community around us, we can begin to understand that we are alike, craving to be accepted, listened to, taken care of, and, most of all, loved. Never underestimate your own beauty and divinity, and know that your life purpose is needed in this world. We are all one and need to be here for each other because we are all in this together.

From now on, I always speak my truth.
I fully embody my authenticity.
Unapologetically.
Completely.
Always with love and compassion.

Healing is on the way.

The Cardinals

The universe never ceases to amaze me when trying times are showing up in my life and I am in need of comfort and peace. When we are open to receiving signs from this overflowing divine source of love without being too attached to the outcome, it is glorious to witness how the energy works for us, delivering the perfect messages of hope that we need most.

Waking up on a Saturday morning, a few days after receiving the cancer diagnosis, I clearly remember asking for a specific sign from my team of guides and angels that would somehow bring me a sense of calm throughout this ordeal. I requested to randomly witness a cardinal bird in any way possible, confirming to me that all would be well even if I was now challenged with this cruel disease.

On that same morning, minutes after quietly asking for the sign in my mind, I dozed off again since my body was still very tired from everything that was going on at the time.

After a while, waking up and still in between worlds, in total disbelief, I heard a very loud chirping sound from a bird outside in the backyard.

Was I still dreaming?

Quickly hopping out of bed, I immediately walked to my bedroom window, astonished to find the sweetest couple of vibrant red cardinal birds perching on the nude branches of our majestic maple tree, which was preparing to blossom. It was the first time I was encountering these gorgeous animals in such a long time. I stayed still, enjoying their beauty and presence for a while until they decided to fly away.

It felt like God was with me and within me, putting a balm on my heart and soothing my deepest fears and anxiety. I felt surrounded by love and healing light, and it was the greatest gift I could wish for, helping me as I traveled through this experience with grace, strength, courage, faith, and the hope I needed for the months to come. I know I am always divinely guided, protected, and unconditionally loved.

And you are too. Remember to ask and be fully open to receiving. The universe is always abundant and magical beyond measure.

It is by going within
in contemplation
with a curious mind
that we finally find
ourselves through
the chaos of life.

Soul-Searching

———

I always belong where my heart
leads me to go.

A flower doesn't judge another.
A flower doesn't compare.
A flower doesn't care if the others
are more vibrant, taller, or sweeter.
A flower just is.
In all its glory.
Fully blooming under the sun.
Perfectly imperfect.

Be like a flower.
Show your authentic self to others.
Without judgment or comparison.
Bloom your unique light to the world.
In all your glory.
Perfect just as you are and have always been.

You are PERFECTLY IMPERFECT.

Look how far you've come.

Celebrate your growth.

My intention today
is remaining intentional
in everything I do.

I choose to focus on
my own frequency.

In stillness, I find the hidden gems
within me that always waited patiently
to be discovered.

Good morning sunshine.
Cheers for a new day.
A new beginning.
A fresh start.
Where new opportunities
and miracles will arise.

Are you open to receive?

―――

Imagine what could be possible if
you would stop doubting yourself.

———

Pure bliss and happiness
come from inner peace.

I forgive myself
for letting anger,
deeply nesting within,
linger for way too long,
like a raging wildfire burning endlessly.
Unpredictable, scorching, and damaging.
Inviting disease in without solicitation.

My body is made of water.
I intend for this pure liquid gold,
nourishing and purifying,
to fully extinguish all remaining blazes
that failed to escape.
I am open, clear, and liberated.

I am whole again.

I hope there are days
when your coffee tastes like magic,
your playlist makes you dance,
strangers make you smile,
and the night sky touches your soul.
I hope you fall in love with being alive again.

—*Brooke Hampton*

I AM Empowered.

I AM Connected.

I AM Kind.

I AM Compassionate.

I AM Lively.

I AM Joyful.

I AM Funny.

I AM Unique.

I AM Rare.

I AM Trustful.

I AM Strong.

I AM Creative.

I AM Expansive.

I AM Magic.

I AM proud to be ME.

I will never feel guilty again
for doing what is best for me.

What belongs to me flows effortlessly
and freely into my life.
I surrender to and stay in a deserving state to receive.
The world is abundant.
There is enough for all of us.
I already believe that it is mine.

I already am holy, perfect,
flawless, and immaculate.

I already am who I always wanted to be.

I already possess everything within me
to design my most authentic and
extraordinary life I've always desired.

I just have to let go of my refusal to believe it.

———

Each day,
I take time for contemplation.
To be in wonder of all the miracles I see,
hear, feel, or taste around me.
I treasure all of it.
I grasp all of it.
I am thankful for all of it.

There are so many things in life to worry about.
What if I choose not to?

If it is not in flow,
there is resistance.

What are you resisting?

Be brave.
Be bold.
Be heroic.
Be adventurous.
Be kindhearted.
Be tender with yourself.

This is who you are.

———

You are limitless.
You truly are.

I am far more capable than I realize.

Speak your truth
with love and compassion.

Always.

Don't worry about how you LOVE.
Don't worry about how you are LOVED.
LOVE is easy.
LOVE is effortless.
LOVE is not complicated.
It is our birthright.
It is who we are.
It is our life's mission.
It is everywhere around us.
In nature.
In the subway.
In hospitals.
In our homes.

LOVE is all around us and LOVE is all that is.

When I surrender, I rise.
When facing a challenge,
there's always a window of opportunity
to surrender without resisting.
It is a lifetime of work.
Every day, I choose to let go
of what I can't control.
I ask to be divinely guided.
I breathe in ease.
I breathe out worry.
I let go.
I set free.
I let God.

And so it is.

~~Social media~~
~~News~~
~~Drama~~

Disconnecting from the outside world
allows me to connect with myself.

My only job is to be authentically ME.
The universe will take care of the rest.

Happiness, ease, peace, and bliss
are not things that live outside of me.
They are something that I already own within my heart.

Dear self,

You are beautiful.
You are magnificent.
You shine light everywhere you go.
You are so loved.
You are always divinely guided.
You are abundant.
You are creative.
You are healthy.
You are whole.
You are supported.
You are exactly where you are supposed to be.
You are unique and perfect.

Do you know how amazing you are?

F False
E Evidence
A Appearing
R Real

I always have free will.
I choose love over fear.

Only love is real.

I always speak to others the way
I want others to speak to me.

I always smile at others the way
I want others to smile at me.

I respect others the way
I want others to respect me.

I love others the way
I want to be loved.

My sanctuary is sacred.
It is a special place where my soul feels at home.
Where I can find my true self.
Despite the upheavals.
Despite the pain, the sadness.
By sitting in stillness
and returning to the heart center.
This portal, I know, I can always access.

I feel at peace, content, and grounded.

———

I will always be
my greatest teacher.

When I share my authenticity
and vulnerability with the world,
I contribute to the healing
of humanity.

I truly evolve when I choose which
emotions I decide to engage with or not.

Breath in with an open heart.
Breath out with an open heart.
Be still with an open heart.
Invite in what you desire with an open heart.
Love with an open heart.
Learn with an open heart.
Lead people with an open heart.

TGIM   Thank God it is Monday
TGIT   Thank God it is Tuesday
TGIW   Thank God it is Wednesday
TGIT   Thank God it is Thursday
TGIF   Thank God it is Friday
TGIS   Thank God it is Saturday
TGIS   Thank God it is Sunday

Be grateful for each day in your life.

They are a precious gift.

Let the past
show you how far
you have come.

Let the present
be a sacred space
of creation and peace.

Let the future
be the mirror of all
the intentions you have made
reflecting into miracles.

A friendly reminder
that we are not a human doing
but a human being.

Take the time to just BE.

It is my birthright to fully
embody who I am.

Unapologetically.

―――

I share my voice and my truth
with love and warmheartedness.

Always.

I am my own guru.
I am my own sage.
I am my own philosopher.

What I am seeking
is already rooted deep within me.

I choose to float gracefully
among the clouds
instead of swimming against
the current of the ocean.

A closed door isn't rejection.
It's a simple detour to something
that is more aligned with where I am.

I trust that something even better
will surface in sacred timing.

Only love is real.
Only love matters.
Love always wins.
Love is all we need.

I am not my fears.
I am not my emotions.
I am not my past.
I am not my mistakes.
I am not my body.
I am a soul, unique and perfect,
learning, growing, and evolving
only for a glimpse in time
before returning home
where I will become one.

I will always try my best
to be the mother to my children
that my inner child always needed.

My sweet soul,
do not rush.

Everything is happening
for your highest good.

Trust the process, my dear.
Your path is the perfect teacher
for your own soul's evolution.

You will rise above the mountains.

Do not rush.

Everything is happening
all in holy timing.

It is okay to feel lost.
It is okay to feel sad.
It is okay to experience darkness.
Never forget that light always wins.
That it is the way.
Tomorrow will be a new day.

Choose to be the light.

It is only a chapter unfolding
from the memoir I am writing.
It is not my whole journey.

I breathe in peace.

I choose to follow my inner compass.
This calm, soft, little voice within.
Guiding me gently every day.
Even if it's uncomfortable.
Knowing, trusting, surrendering
to her guidance.
Always for my highest good.

I am not sorry for saying no.
I am not sorry for putting myself first.
I am not sorry for choosing myself over others.
I am not sorry for speaking my truth.
I am not sorry for filling my cup.
I am not sorry for resting.
I am not sorry for being in solitude.
I am not sorry for being me.

All of me.

———

My intention today is remaining intentional in everything I do.

Today I choose to:

walk in my truth,
conquer my fears,
speak with love,
lead with compassion,
not be angry,
not worry,
not judge,
live fearlessly,
welcome my emotions,
witness my inner beauty,
and witness my inner strength.

I am grateful to be alive.

It is okay to not know what is next.
It is okay to be at peace until the answer comes.

I surrender knowing that all is well.

I met God at a coffee shop
on this chilly fall Monday morning
while waiting in line at the drive-thru,
tired, impatient, and in a hurry to get to work
like many others starting a new week.

Arriving at the window,
I remember the friendly barista telling me
that the person in front of me
already paid for my coffee.

My heart flooded with love.
My heart exploded with joy.

This act of kindness on that chilly Monday morning
changed my perspective and my day.

In a second, my fatigue changed into vitality.
My impatience transformed into harmony.

I decided to pay it forward and do the same act
of kindness to the individual in the car behind me.
You never know how a simple act of kindness
can impact a person's life.

The message here for everyone is
that you can find kindness in everyone.

God is within everything.
God is within everyone.
God is everywhere.

Today, I remind myself:

to breathe,
to stop,
to take time for self-care,
to love wholeheartedly,
to move my body,
to create,
to smile,
to laugh,
to rest,
to be brave.

To just be authentically ME.

FEAR is not our worst enemy.
FEAR is our most sacred teacher.

Always present, realigning our spirit,
on the path to LOVE.

———

Make every day
a ME day.

Fill your own cup.

Self-care is <u>nonnegotiable</u>.

In a deep inhale,
I invite peace.
In a deep exhale,
I invite peace.

In a deep inhale,
I invite unconditional love.
In a deep exhale,
I invite unconditional love.

In a deep inhale,
I invite healing.
In a deep exhale,
I invite healing.

In a deep inhale,
I invite abundance.
In a deep exhale,
I invite abundance.

In a deep inhale,
I invite joy.
In a deep exhale,
I invite joy.

In a deep inhale,
I invite bliss.
In a deep exhale,
I invite bliss.

How can I give myself more love today?
How can I be nicer to myself today?
How can I help my body heal today?
How can I receive more today?
How can I experience more joy today?
How can I be of service today?

How can my light shine brighter today?

By healing myself,
I heal the people
who came before me,
the people around me,
and the people who
will come after me.

Healing

In March 2022,
I was brought to my knees
from a phone call that changed my life.

"You have CANCER."

Feeling powerless, lost, scared, and numb.
Unworthy, disgusted, sad.
Who had I become
with this disease
that was living in my body?
Why was this happening to me?

I've shed all the tears I had in my body until the well was empty.
I've felt all the feelings that were emerging deeply from within.
My body was communicating with me.
I chose to transform this into beauty.
I chose to shift the pain into transformation.

On this Earth school,
it was a lesson I had chosen
to heal in a profound way.
Becoming wiser and stronger.

Remembering who I was on the first day
my soul was born into this world.

Whole, unique, and perfect.

To my sweet little butterfly,

Today is Saturday.
The last Saturday embodying you, little butterfly.
I thank you for everything you did for me throughout my life.
I am sorry that illness has nested around your beautiful wings.
Oh, how this has taught me so much.
It is now your time to rest.
A transformation is emerging within me.
I am keeping you energetically and lovingly alive.
Your wings will remain,
healthy and stronger than ever,
working your magic perfectly
from a new dimension.
You will never be gone. You will never be forgotten.
My body is balanced and only healthy cells are present.
I love you . . . please know that.
Spread your wings and fly.

I am forever grateful for you.

It will be painful for a while.
It will be uncomfortable for a while.
It will be challenging for a while.

Reaching the peak of the mountain
I've been climbing for many months
with perseverance and strength.

Peace and calm prevailed.
I've ascended and triumphed.
Freedom and healing are here.

I release.

I release.

I release.

I release.

I release.

I surrender completely.

I am free.

I keep going.
I keep growing.
I keep healing.

I am proud of how far I've come.
Of what I've survived.
I can do so much more.
I believe in me.

Always and forever.

Somewhere in my life,
I've lost my way.
Cancer has been my savior,
slowing time,
making the space for soul-searching
and contemplation,
a mirror reflecting back to me
what is required to liberate and set free.

Cancer has been this precious guiding light
leading the way so I could find myself again.

In this healing process,
I choose to shift the pain into power
and my wounds into wisdom.

I honor the spark of the divine within me.
I am so much more powerful than my
human brain can comprehend.
I come from an infinite source of unconditional love.
I am here to share my unique, multifaceted light with the world.
My soul is magnificent and limitless,
reaching the stars, the cosmos, and the galaxies.

Wholeness is already here and who I am.

Releasing all past traumas
that have been haunting me for many years.
Peeling them, layer by layer.
I am shedding my old skin,
welcoming new beginnings.

I am liberated.

Sitting with my feelings.
Observing them quietly.
Acknowledging them.
Free of judgment or shame.
They are my own unique compass
coming through softly in my awareness
to gently communicate what I need to know,
so it can be processed and let go.
Sitting with my feelings.
Getting to know them.
To love them.
To be grateful for them.
I am learning to understand
the whispers of my soul
that are guiding me quietly
to my divine essence.

I am so amazed and
mesmerized by my body's ability
to heal, restore, and regenerate
naturally, effortlessly,
beautifully, and magically.

This life-force energy
that restores the old,
that transforms disease
into ease and wholeness.

My body is unique,
ethereal, sublime, and perfect.
I know it always has my back.

I love it more and more
each day, and I promise
I will always care, listen,
and protect it.

To the parts of me I've left behind,
thank you for showing me
what needed to be healed,
so I can become whole again.

I am limitless.
I create my unique experience.
It's never too late to start afresh.
I trust the process.

Knowing I am powerful
and divinely directed.

I have a fire within me
that can never be extinguished.

It is fierce,
wild,
mighty,
magical,
ethereal.

Eternal.

―――

I am bent
but not broken.

I am small
but almighty.

Magic is everywhere.
I always look for the signs around me.
A beautiful bird perching on the window.
A song I hear reminding me of a loved one.
A smile from a stranger when I feel down.
A hug from my child when I feel hopeless.
A scenic sunset sparkling in the water to ease my worries.

The universe supports me every day.
I just have to be open to receive.
I go inward for inspiration and messages.
Magic is everywhere.

I AM magic.

I am learning how to unlearn
what I've been taught that
doesn't serve me anymore.

I am limitless.
I truly am.

Surrendering completely and
letting go of all the expectations
I have about the outcome
is one of the most precious gifts
this disease has given me.

I choose love.
I choose peace.
I choose joy.
I choose myself.

―――

I am the greatest love
of my life.

―――

I don't know what tomorrow will have in store for me.
I intend to fully be present
in this exact moment,
where I have the power to materialize
the future that is most aligned
with my unique life purpose.

I trust in myself.

I trust the universe.

I bow to my body with reverence
for its capacity to heal
naturally and perfectly.
For its strength and resilience
I didn't even know it had.

I bow to you with complete reverence.

Thank you for keeping me safe, healthy, and alive.

———

I go inward.

This is where my true power lies.

Even in the most tumultuous times,
I know that hope is always in front of me.
I choose to take it one step at a time
and trust that all is perfectly and divinely
planned for my highest good.

All is perfectly well.

2022 is my summer of healing.
A time of contemplation.
A time of reflection.
A time of introspection.

I welcome all past traumas
to resurface in this present moment.
Embodying fully in the uncomfortable.
Allowing space to dig deep
into the depths of my core self.
I release all anger, fear, and resentment
that no longer serve me anymore.

I choose to surround myself with
peace, bliss, love, and ease.

As a woman who heals herself,
I heal all the women in my lineage
who came before and after me.

I heal my grandmother,
I heal my mother,
I heal my daughter,
and I heal all the women around me.

How beautiful it is.

———

It is okay to take as much time as I need
to heal myself.

Slowly.
Peacefully.
Gracefully.

It is OK to not figure
everything out right now.

It is OK for me to not know
what's coming next.

Healing takes time.
One step in front of the other.

All in divine timing.
Better days are coming my way.

To the parts of me I've left behind,
thank you for showing me
the skin I had to shed.
The unhealthy thoughts and patterns
I had to let go.

I am grateful for your precious
teachings and gifts.

———

I am proud of how far I've come.

Through all the challenges I have faced.
Through all the tears I have shed.
Through all the hardships I have overcome.
I am stronger than I think.
There is nothing I can't be or accomplish.

I am a warrior.
I am a survivor.
I am a thriver.

Just breathe.

All is well.

———

I only let in:

Love

Compassion

Joy

Abundance

Laughter

Passion

Peace

Bliss

Ease

I now choose to paint outside the lines
I'd once drawn for myself many years ago.

I find the courage to free myself and welcome
any hidden creations and possibilities
that come my way with open arms and an open heart.

―――

I feel lighter.
Light as the air.

I breathe deeply.
Without constriction.

I fill my body with love and light.
I feel lighter.

Like a bird flying away from its nest.
Like a butterfly emerging from its chrysalis.

I am light. I am liberated.

I was scared of the unknown
until I surrendered my fear to the universe.

I believed in my strength, my resilience,
and how powerful I was.

I had been given everything I needed
to win any battle that life threw on my path.

Liberating everything that was keeping me small and fearful.
Transforming myself into my most authentic self.

Multiplying my light everywhere I went.
Enlightening the world around me.

I felt tranquility within.

Laughter has been my dearest and most precious companion I could have throughout my healing process.

I give gratitude to the disease for:

Engaging a deeper connection with my body.
The chance to pause and restore.
Showing me how to love myself deeply.
Teaching me how to be kinder to myself.
Opening up space for self-care and healing.
Guiding me to release stored emotions.
Leading the way for me to forgive others and myself.
Showing me that I am strong and resilient.
Having more compassion for myself.
Making time to meditate and reconnect within.
Redirecting me to my highest self.

I send love to my soul.
I send love to my body.
I send love to my inner child.
I send love to all living things.
I send love to my ancestors who paved the way before me.
I send love to the sick and the poor around the world.
I send love to everything that is made of fear.
I release all trauma and send it love.

I am whole.

Through suffering, there is always
an avenue for releasing, healing,
awakening, and finding enlightenment
if I decide to fully participate in the process.

It is an occasion to love more, trust more,
to take risks, and know exactly who I am.

———

I will never be ashamed of my scars.
Like a tattoo, they will be a lifetime souvenir that
I am stronger than the disease that
tried to break me.

A message to myself:

I am so proud of you.
I love you so much.

If trauma can be passed down
through generations
then so can healing.

—@medicine_mami

Slow and soft healing is a beautiful process
that should be celebrated too.

Sometimes this is what our soul may need
to evolve and expand into its highest potential.

My unique frequency
is a gift to the world.

I consciously use this gift
wisely and with love.

Collectively, we will raise
the frequency of the world,
crafting a blissful haven
for our future generations.

I let go of stress.
I let go of control.
I let go of tension.
I let go of anger.
I let go of resentment.
I let go of guilt.
I let go of sadness.
I let go of old limitations.
I let go of old patterns.
I let go. I let go. I let go.

I am at peace with the process.
I am at peace with myself.

I come back home.

Healing requires letting go and allowing the unknown to take place.

Surrendering creates space for miracles.

Every healing hand that will be
in contact with me during and after surgery
will be an extension of God's hands.
The surgery will go through effortlessly and perfectly.
I will recover quickly and comfortably.
Every day, I will feel better and stronger.
My mind, body, and spirit are balanced and well.

Thank you.
Thank you.
Thank you.

A sacred pause:

To restore.
To regenerate.
To recharge.
To recover.
To recuperate.
To reevaluate.
To reflect.
To heal.

A time of gratitude.
A time to bathe in stillness.
A time to welcome peace.
A time to be fully present.
A time to be kind to myself.

It is okay if I don't figure
everything out for what
will be coming next.

I just have to trust that
what happens will be
for my soul's highest good,
growth, and evolution.

———

Hello fear.

I am listening to you.
I am seeing you.
I am feeling you.
Without criticism.
With total admiration and tenderness.
I thank you for keeping me safe
through all these years.
I am blessing you.

I free you.

I liberate the heavy burden
I've been carrying from my past,
welcoming a lighter state of being.
In this present moment,
I am opening this sacred space
to create the destiny
I've been longing and craving for
deep within me.

———

I release any control.
I release any expectations
about how my healing process
should be unfolding.

I trust this infinite wisdom
that lives within me
to restore, recalibrate, and cure
my body perfectly and
for my own greatest good.

I am loved and supported.
I let go.
I let GOD.

And so it is.

I honor and love every part of my strong and healthy body.
Every cell is luminous, filled with energy and vitality.
My intention is my reality.
I feel it deeply within my body,
memorizing this feeling,
releasing my intention to the universe.
I am perfect.
I am complete.

I surrender.

I open my eyes to all the beauty around me.
I open my ears to all who need to be listened to.
I open my arms to everyone who needs me.
I open my heart to all the love surrounding me.

What if everything I was going through at this moment was preparing me for everything I've always asked to receive?

―――

One day at a time.

I am not the same person
I was last month or a year ago.
My soul is transforming and
blossoming into a higher state of being.

Understanding my truth
with a better perspective.

Accepting my strengths and
weaknesses without judgment.

Knowing my limits physically and
emotionally without shame.

A return to wholeness.

―――

Let it flow.
Let it be.

Trust the process.

I choose who enters my inner space.
I decide who I give my energy to.

———

I choose to use my energy to believe,
trust, deepen, and heal.
I choose not to worry.
My path is not hard for me.
It is mine and I know I am guided and
protected with every step I take.
I release any resistance, and
I am grateful for this moment of
change and expansion.
Healing is a deep journey back to self.

Back to love.

By changing small things around me,
I make space for new things to manifest
internally within me.

Healing creates space for:

Transformation.
Transmutation.
Reflection.
Remembering.
Releasing.
Unbecoming.
Softening.
Deepening.

A return to self.

Nature was our medicine
before we had medicine.

Grounding.
Nurturing.
Comforting.
Healing.

To all the suppressed emotions
I've let enter into my physical body.
Unprocessed. Voiceless.

I see you.
I forgive you.
I understand you.
I am grateful for you.
I release you.
I love you.

Unconditionally.

I only let in space in my life for:

Love
Light
Happiness
Laughter
Curiosity
Healing
Passion
Creativity
Peace
Calm

Healing
steadily,
beautifully,
softly,
peacefully
at my own pace,
with empathy
and unconditional love.

It is the most precious gift
I can offer myself.

In complete stillness,
a caterpillar was born,
transformed from my former self,
emerging from the chrysalis
as a magnificent butterfly.
Softly unfolding my wings,
I become alive and new.

God, help me go through this challenge with ease,
grace, peace, acceptance, and absolute love.
Thank you for your guidance, devotion, and loving presence.
Healing is my birthright, and I know I can win this.

Give me the strength to stay positive and find the
hidden treasures beneath it all.
I want to experience as little pain as possible and be
comfortable throughout the process.

I am open to any spiritual, emotional, mental, and
physical healing I need at this time. I trust the process.
I know this is all for my highest good.

Disease in my body is an invitation
for me to dive deep into my own healing
and reorder my life only with what brings me joy.

―――

Rainy days are temporary.
I am a work in progress.
A multifaceted being always learning and evolving.
I welcome all the healing available to me.
I am already whole and healthy.
I know the sun will rise tomorrow.

In that I fully trust.

In this next chapter, I will:

Manifest intentionally what I want.
Do what brings me joy.
Step into my power without shame.
Shine my light brightly.
Prioritize radical self-care.
Invite peace, love, and healing every day.
Create more space for what excites me.
Fill my cup first before giving my energy to others.
Know when to say no when my heart leads me to do so.
Learn to say yes when my soul guides me to do so.
Respect my time, my space, and my energy.
Live fearlessly.

―――

It is safe for me to speak my truth.
To share my voice without shame or guilt.

I MATTER.
I AM WHOLE.
I AM LOVED.

I allow healing light to flow
through my entire body,
shifting and restoring all the cells and organs
that need love, healing, and care.
I trust in my own ability to heal my physical body.
I allow the healing I need to arise in a deep cellular level.
I give space for this healing to occur by
being fully present in my body.

May this divine light shift everything
that is out of alignment into wholeness.

―――

Everything in my life is divinely guided.
I am at peace knowing that everything
is perfectly orchestrated for my highest good.
I give thanks to the universe for leading me
toward a miraculous outcome.

I trust the process.

I surrender to love.

―――

I inhale love, peace, joy, health, and bliss.
I exhale anger, resentment, and fear.

Repeat.

I allow everything to flow freely within me.

Releasing any resistance I may have.

Deeply feeling the discomfort.

Breathing into it until it has passed.

Peeling the many layers accumulated with the years.

Accepting changes without any expectation.

Opening my heart to boundless love.

Remaining in the present moment.

Feeling appreciation for all I've been through.

I am safe.

I am loved.

I let go.

Resistance is fading away.

My heart is blooming gracefully.

Without judgment, I liberate attachment.

I am gentle, patient, and kind to myself.

I surround myself with joy and ease.

I surrender to the process.

It is only a phase, a cycle, a season.

I allow myself to feel everything.

Elevating to a higher vibration.

Embodying the newer version of me I have become.

Like a butterfly emerging from its chrysalis.

Being reborn, ready for a new start,

in an enchanted world full of hope.

Healing is not a destination
but an intense, vibrant, chaotic,
turbulent voyage revealing to me
the essence of who I truly am.

Pure and divine.

I remember my own holiness.

I speak my truth with love.

I express myself unrestrainedly without shame.

I let my inner child play without fear.

I create beauty all around me.

I listen to my body and inner compass.

I practice letting go, surrendering fully.

I surround myself with positivity.

I always fill my cup first.

I look in the mirror and see the perfect divine being I am.

I only invite love, peace, and joy around me.

Today, I have the courage to break,
release, and let go of all old patterns
and limiting beliefs in my life,
that have always kept me small and
are not serving me anymore,
for my highest good and who I have become.
Thank you for showing me where I need healing.

I bless you.
I release you.

―――

I am safe in my body.
My body is my temple.
My body is my sanctuary.
My body is my oasis.
My presence is my power.
It is a blessing to others.
My body is strong.
My body is resilient
My body is intelligent.
My mind is at ease.
I radiate love.
I embody peace.
My body communicates perfectly.
I am truly taken care of.

My body is MIRACULOUS.

It is a period of transition.
It is a time of transformation.
I now move out of my own way.
To be shown the right path.
I trust the guidance.
I take a leap of faith.
A door to greatness is opening.
A new journey begins.
I allow it to be simple.

Powerful.
Blissful.
Magical.

Shifting my focus out of my head
and dropping it into my heart
is the most potent act of self-love
I can provide myself throughout
my healing journey.

———

I celebrate myself:

For being ME.
For being REAL.
For being UNAPOLOGETIC.
For being RAW.
For being AUTHENTIC.

For all the progress I have made.

I am so proud.

Vibrate in your TRUTH always.
May all blockages be released.

Physically.
Emotionally.
Mentally.
Spiritually.

May your body be restored.
Replenished.
Whole again.

May you be divinely guided
in the process.

Healing can be messy, raw, and uncomfortable.
It can be exquisite and transformative.
It can be quiet.
It can be loud.
It can be quick.
It can take time.
We cannot rush it.
It is not a race.
It has to be . . . at our own pace.

Believe that all will unravel perfectly.

My scars are badges of strength and courage.

They tell a story.

About my pain.
About courage.
About perseverance.
About rebirth.
Unique and raw.
Adorning my body like a tattoo.
Accompanying me for the rest of my life.
And reminding me of who I was, who I am,
and who I will become.

Peace is surrendering to what I can't control.
Training my mind to live life as it is.
Not the way I think it should be.
Surrendering so the universe can lead the way.
Knowing that all is happening for my highest good.

I am peace.

Peace is within me.

Peace is all around me.

Breathe in. Breathe out.
Say hello to your body.
Your body craves your attention.
Connect fully with your body.
Feeling the energy pulsing, moving, and circulating.
Stay in this for a while.
Are you feeling any tension, pain, emotions, or discomfort?
Stay with it. Be with it. In complete presence.
Are you feeling at peace?
Stay with it. Be with it. No judgment, just complete presence.
Thank your body for being the perfectly designed vessel.
Embodying, comforting your soul at this moment in time.
Your body needs attention.
It needs self-care and unconditional love.
To be respected, to be nourished, to be listened to.

Our bodies communicate with us.
Are you listening?

The wound is the gift.
A lifetime memento
of the woman I was before,
the woman I am today,
and the woman I will become.

It is a gift of growth.
A gift of expansion.
A gift of transformation.

It is a reminder of my inner strength.
A reminder of my resilience.
Of sharing my truth.
Of choosing myself first.

Forty-four trips around the sun,
I am finding my way back home.
Mutating and emerging from the dark.
Facing my shadow.
Reclaiming my own truth.
Letting go of who I am not anymore.
Welcoming my new identity.

Through suffering, hardships, and struggles,
I expand my wings.
Entirely trusting myself.
Returning to love.

I hold space for my emotions to come through,
giving them permission to express freely
without shame or judgment.
May I find peace
in the discomfort that may arise.
I let them pass by
as a messenger of love.
I am grateful for what I've learned from them.

I offer myself forgiveness:

For how I may have treated myself in the past.
For how I may have shamed myself in the past.
For how I may have not honored myself in the past.
For how I may have doubted myself in the past.
For speaking poorly to myself in the past.
For not loving myself wholly in the past.

I am sorry.
Please forgive me.
Thank you.
I love you.

―――

Cancer is unsettling.

Perturbing.

Uncomfortable.

Scary.

Heavy on my chest.

Transforming.

Grounding.

Life changing.

Heart opening.

A return to self.

Treat yourself with:

Tenderness.
Humility.
Humbleness.
Love.
Delicacy.

Be gentle with yourself.

And others will follow.

Time heals all wounds.

How magnificent is my body.
Healing gracefully on its own.
By this intelligent loving source.
On its perfectly natural pace.

This force of nature.
That keeps my heart beating.
Without any intention from my part.
Restoring each cell into light.

I give thanks to the universe
for her miracles.

For my life.

To my ancestors.

To all the women who came before me.

I honor your journey, your ordeals, your strength.

I liberate trauma from our lineage.

Making space for a new path to forge before me.

For the generations that will succeed me.

I feel gratitude to be alive in this present moment.

I am willing to do the work. All of it.

Grounding this new energy into Mother Earth.

I trust my divine path.

We are all healing, releasing, recalibrating, restructuring.

Restoring and realigning to who we are.

Sacred and divine, I stand in my truth.

With all of you by my side.

We are all one.

Healed and whole.

I choose to release fear.
I choose to release anger.
I choose to release judgment.
I choose to release procrastination.
I choose to release resentment.

I choose to focus on what brings me joy.

I choose LOVE.

I honor my healing journey.
I honor my ancestors.
I honor my mistakes.
I honor my teachers.
I honor my challenges.
I honor my experiences.
I honor my failures.
I honor my accomplishments.
I honor my triggers.
I honor my resilience.
I honor myself with love.

I bow to the forest that welcomed me
to recharge and ground my energy.
I bow to the trees that shared their knowledge with me.
I bow to the wind for allowing me to release
what is not serving me anymore.
I bow to the flowers for showing me how beautiful
and magnificent our home is.
I bow to the crow for teaching me its wisdom.
I bow to the turtle for inviting me to slow down.
I bow to the ground that connects me with Mother Earth.
I bow to the sky for guiding me every day without limitations.
I bow to the water for replenishing my body with
life-force energy.

I bow to Mother Nature for being
my greatest teacher and healer.

―――

I am an empathic being.
I am a compassionate being.
I am a sensitive being.

I am LOVE.

―――

In life, some things have to end
to make space for better things to begin.

I set free and let go of who
I've always thought I was.
Embodying entirely
who I truly am.

———

My dear inner child.

When did I decide to separate myself from you?
When did I decide to not trust myself completely?
When did I forget that life didn't have to be complicated?
When did I forget to feel safe?

My dear inner child.
I hear you. I see you. I understand you.
It is safe to let go and be free.

You are perfect.
You are free.
You are loved.

I witness all my pain, aching,
symptoms, and suffering.

My body's language has been
suppressed for way too long.

I acknowledge my feelings without judgment
and with complete understanding.

I now free myself of the past,
welcoming a fresh start.

Feeling emotional in every level of my being.

Afraid, exhausted, helpless.

Tired of waiting. Tired of the unknown.

Of the solitude in a time of a pandemic.

I've cried all the tears I could until my reserve went dry.

Screaming at the top of my lungs.

Alone in my room.

I am done. I am done. I am done.

Knowing that an angel is standing right beside me.

Surrounding me with his wings.

I surrender to the present moment.

Feeling a sense of peace.

An indescribable quiet, a release.

In that instant, I chose to thank these tears.

For softening the pain.

A return to love.

All over again.

Understanding forgiveness
has been one of the most profound lessons
I've acquired in this transformational healing journey,
freeing myself of resentment,
of anger, and of false interpretation from my mind.

I feel weightless.

———

I forgive myself.
I forgive myself.
I forgive myself.

I forgive myself.
I forgive myself.
I forgive myself.

I love you.

Thank you to my higher self
for bringing me back to who I am.

One day you will tell your story
of how you overcame what you're going
through right now.

—*Mel Robbins*

I've been running a marathon
in my mind, my body, and my soul.

It has been hard.
It has been painful.
It has been tiring.

But I've been tenacious
and courageous.
With only a few miles to go,
I can finally perceive the finish line.

I am proud of my progress.
I am proud of my accomplishments.
I can now rest for a while.
Now the race is over.

I am perfect.
All is well.

―――

Today,

I celebrate my life.
I celebrate my wins.
I celebrate my failures.
I celebrate the woman I am.
I celebrate my strength.
I celebrate my losses.
I celebrate how far I've come.

I am going to
make everything
around me beautiful.
That will be my life.

—*Elsie De Wolfe*

Emerging

I am a soulful artist.
Creating my own unique masterpiece.
Inspiring love, beauty, and the divine feminine.
Diving deeper into the core of my soul.
I become the creator of my own destiny.

———

I am a quiet leader and
in my presence:

I inspire.
I lead.
I create.
I love.
I nurture.
I heal.

The goddess within me is:

A teacher.
A mother.
A daughter.
Powerful.
Magnificent.
Beautiful.
Celestial.
Compassionate.
A survivor.
A healer.
A lightworker.
A believer.
A conqueror.
A creator.

INFINITE.

I only choose to speak the language of love
since it is the only language of truth that exists.

I allow love to radiate everywhere around me.
I allow abundance to flow endlessly into my life.
I allow new friendships to flourish beautifully.
I allow my challenges to make me stronger.
I allow my anger to show me where I need more love.
I allow fear to show me where I need healing.

I choose to let go of who I think I am
to create space to become my true self.

We all have this remarkable ability
to change, to mutate and recreate
our lives no matter how crazy and
frightening it may seem.

We should always have faith that there is
a better version of ourselves on the other side,
waiting to be discovered.

You are the only person with
the power to rewrite your story.

You can always recreate
your experience.

You are never too old,
and it's never too late to start again.

Creating is my purpose.
Creating is my medicine.
Beauty is the language of love.
I inspire beauty everywhere I go.

When I create, I feel connected.
When I create, I feel alive.
When I create, I heal myself.
When I create, I heal others.

I create more balance in my life.

I make more time for self-love and self-care.

I respect my own limits and boundaries.

I live boldly and chase my wildest dreams without limits.

I invite love, beauty, and magic into my space.

I serve God in my most authentic way.

Everything in my life is about creating beauty.

Raising the frequency.

In a real, grounded way.

Through art, writing, and the energy I hold around me.

Creating through love.

Healing through love.

Breathing in love.

Breathing out love.

I want to infuse love in everything I do.

In everything I am.

It is the energy I leave behind.

———

I am a creator.
I am a magician.
I am a witch.
I am an artist.
I am a manifestor.
I am a sorcerer.
I am a healer.
I am a teacher.

I AM.

There is a talent within me that only I possess.
A unique and direct connection to my own muse.
Always whispering inspiring ideas in my ears.
That only I can birth and share into this world.

The world needs my uniqueness.

I will do the things
that excite me,
that inspire me,
that scare me,
that give me meaning
and purpose.

By creating better boundaries around me,
I make space for peace and tranquility to arise within me.

Releasing any anger or resentment
I may have kept inside for too long.

I respect my needs, my limits, and my energy reserve,
so my cup can become full again.

I will always be my greatest project.

Nothing haunts us like the things we don't say.

—*Mitch Albom*

I surrender to the past.
I surrender to the present.
I surrender to the future.

I trust that everything
is happening for me,
all in divine timing and
for my greatest good.

The Last Mile

Journal entries and daily musings from
the very last mile of my cancer journey

October 31

My husband has been running marathons for more than a decade, and I have a pretty good idea of what is needed from an athlete to accomplish a race, from the training process to passing through the finish line. Passion, resilience, commitment, focus, confidence, and a strong desire to reach the end are all essential components for success. During the whole cancer journey, I truly felt I was required to put myself in the skin of a marathoner. I had to be passionate to learn as much as possible about the disease by being involved in finding the tools and care for a hopefully successful outcome. I also had to be mentally and emotionally resilient to face the pain and all of my fears of the surgery, radiation treatment, and the unknown. I needed to commit and focus on my goals of healing completely and returning to wholeness again. And finally, I had to be confident in myself, my medical team, and the universe that whatever I was going through was here to show me a lesson, guiding me gently on my highest path and reminding me of how unshakable my body and soul are.

As I am writing these words, I am currently on my last mile. Near the finish line. As proud as I've always been of my husband when he finished a race, I have so much pride in how I was able to venture this journey with grace and resilience, turn this obscure experience into a transformative one, and find the light at the end of the tunnel.

We always have to remember that the light always wins.

Light is what we are made of.

We are pure and indestructible.

November 1

Yesterday was the last day of the month of October. Halloween is now over, and I am sure we will have enough candy to eat until Christmas. On the first day of November, I always feel a change of energy, like the beginning of a new year. This year, it felt very special. Well, for me anyway. I've been waiting for this month to come for such a long time. Since last March, so much has happened.

Between all the doctors' appointments, blood tests, multiple scans, the surgery, the adjustment to my new medication, and mostly, feeling exhausted from an iron deficiency, fatigue, and anxiety of the unknown. It has been a long ride, and I am excited that the marathon I've been running for the past six months is coming to an end.

I don't know what will be next in my new chapter, but I feel like this race has been such a powerful experience, and I hope that the new path will be smoother than the former one. When I woke up this morning, I set the intention that the last step in this healing process would be soft and kind to me. I've been on a low-iodine diet for the past two weeks and will be until two days after my treatment. Next week will be my last sprint. On Monday and Tuesday, November 7 and 8, I will need to prepare my body for radiation by receiving two Thyrogen injections in my arm and having one last blood test before the treatment.

The day after, on November 9, I will finally be taking my radioactive iodine pill, which will only target my throat area and hopefully destroy all remaining cancerous cells if there are any left from after the surgery. It will truly be a test of faith and surrendering. After the treatment, I cannot be in physical contact with anyone for two days and will have to isolate in my room, reducing the chance of exposing my family to the radiation, and will have to isolate from the world around me in my home for a total of five days.

This too seems like déjà vu after going through three years of a long pandemic. Some uncomfortable side effects could be felt for six weeks or more after the treatment, including headaches, nausea, swelling of my salivary glands, dry mouth, fatigue, and so on. I pray that it will go effortlessly, and on November 14, I will finally undergo a two-hour-long body scan to determine if there are still traces of the cancer or if it has completely left my physical body at this point in remission.

So many thoughts are twirling and dancing around inside my head right now, but again, I choose to focus on how I've been unbreakable and still am. I know I can do this, and there is always light at the end of the tunnel, the same way the sun always shines after the rain. I am still learning to grow and let go of what I don't have control over. It is truly a lifelong journey, but I trust in God and I trust in myself, who is as mighty as my creator.

November 4

It has been such a beautiful and unusual November morning. It was 15 degrees Celsius outside in Ottawa. Warmer than all the previous years, I went for my ritual morning walk with no coat on, letting all the sun's vitamins penetrate my skin. Listening to Ella Fitzgerald and Louis Armstrong on a loop, I felt genuinely thankful for both of their soothing voices in my ears. They have been important allies for the past few months, calming my nervous mind from all the constant turbulence that had been going on, even if for a brief moment.

Escaping from reality has definitely been a challenge this year, but taking one day at a time, surrendering, and trusting all my wonderful medical team has helped me remain hopeful of becoming whole again.

November 7

Waking up, I felt excited but apprehensive. Today was the first day of four medical appointments scheduled this week. Before taking the radioactive iodine pill, I needed to receive two Thyrogen injections that had the task of tricking my body into thinking I was not taking my thyroid medication for the treatment to increase its effectiveness. After spending three hours at the hospital, waiting for a blood test, and getting my shot, we finally arrived home. Feeling extremely fatigued and nauseous, I went upstairs and took a well-deserved nap and drank some lemon and ginger water to ease my upset stomach.

I know this is all happening for my highest good, and I am hopeful for the best outcome.

November 8

Today was the BIG day. I finally received my radioactive iodine treatment this afternoon at 1:30 p.m. The Thyrogen injections felt way worse than expected. My hormones were through the roof, and I was left feeling completely worn out, along with an upset stomach. It was definitely not a very pleasant experience, but I knew I had to go through all of it so the cancer could finally, and hopefully, leave my body for good.

While waiting for the doctor and nurse to come and administer the treatment for me, I noticed a little cup filled with water on the table at my left. I then had the impulse to take it in both of my hands and visualize the water being filled with healing energy, with the intention for the treatment to work successfully. I imagined the radioactive pill like a rainbow of healing light entering my body and restoring each and every cancerous cell to health.

I feel such pride and comfort knowing that the last mile to health is getting closer. I've made a promise to myself to never lose hope, even in times of pain and incertitude. I've already gone through so much in the past nine months, and I know I can do this no matter what.

I cannot hide that I also had many moments when I just wanted to quit. From time to time, disruptive thoughts were lurking around me, trying to scare me. I am only human, and I know that all the feelings I've been experiencing were such a significant part of my healing process. I will continue to treat myself with kindness and love without judgment or expectations, and watching some cheerful series on Netflix will surely not hurt.

November 14

The time showing up on my clock this morning when I woke up from a dream was 4:44 a.m. The number four has always been my lucky number since I was a child, and it is also known to have the same wavelength as the vibration of the angels. How amazing it was to receive such a powerful message on the morning of my scan. It was the perfect sign the universe could send me at this time. In that instant, I knew everything would be okay, whatever the results would show on the scans. I felt at peace and, again, decided to surrender and choose to focus on what was bringing me joy.

Getting out of the hospital after a two-hour-long full body 3D scan, it definitely felt like stepping on the finish line after a long, exhausting, and tumultuous race. I felt proud and relieved that I had done everything I could to hopefully have a clean bill of health. Like any marathoner running their last mile, I had to push through all my pain and discomforts along the way to be able to complete the race.

When my journey started, this last mile seemed so far away and unattainable. I continue to be grateful for the support I've received from all the people around me. I feel so much more compassionate self-love and respect for the woman I am now and for who I've always been. I have no words to explain how I am amazed at my ability to restore, regenerate, and self-heal.

My body is a miracle, and I am very grateful for this unique, intelligent vehicle I was born into, allowing me to explore and live life to its fullest in this moment in time on planet Earth.

November 20

On this crisp and chilly morning, I felt a comforting wave of peace washing over my entire body while I was walking in the fresh glittering snow that had just fallen on the ground the night before. Looking at the bright blue sky above me, I had this knowing that everything would be okay, no matter what my scan results would be. I understood that whatever the outcome would be, I was prepared to face it with grace and openness, as I did when I was first diagnosed.

November 22

Waiting for the results from my scan, I felt a little bit more energy than usual and decided to go out and about looking for some wool to crochet a new blanket to curl up with near the fire this winter. The thyroid gland has a very important role in controlling our body's temperature, and since mine had been removed, I knew it would be a little more challenging for me to keep my body warm and cozy this upcoming season.

On my way to the art supply store, I was driving behind a burgundy red car that was moving forward very slowly. A red light appeared in front of us, and as I waited for the light to turn green again, I casually glanced at the license plate of the car. With elation, chills ran down every part of my body from head to toe. The last three numbers on the plate were 999.

The spiritual meaning of the number 999 signifies completion. A sign to move on. A point of closure. How exceptional and on point it was, seeing this number on the car in front of me days after I'd had my final body scan and was waiting for the results.

Exactly like the cardinals that appeared at my window in the beginning of this journey, and exactly eight months after my diagnosis, another beautiful sign had been delivered. Everything has always been perfectly aligned with what my soul needed at the moment.

November 30

Today, I am feeling grateful and excited that tomorrow afternoon, on December 1, I will finally have my whole-body scan results from my wonderful and talented surgeon. My physical vessel can't stand in place, and my mind is racing full speed, very similar to when I received the call on the cancer diagnosis, which marked the start of this rocky adventure. Tomorrow will hopefully mark its ending.

I now feel closer to the finish line, but healing is never over. It is a lifetime practice, but each bump on the road is a possibility to learn to become better, wiser, and kinder to ourselves. This ending will mark a fresh start where everything will be possible—a new opportunity to live life to its fullest, carry less emotional weight on my back, and make space to share my voice with more ease and peace.

I inhale peace. I exhale peace. And so it is.

December 1

Today was THE DAY. I felt excited and nervous, but the only control I had in this situation was surrendering my fears to God and directing my energy intentionally toward a positive outcome.

Waiting, hopefully for the last time in the hospital's ENT department, my hands were moist and my heart was beating swiftly. Having my husband by my side, hand in hand, calmed my nerves greatly. It was late in the afternoon, and the room was almost empty. The clock was ticking so very slowly. I've been used to this waiting game, and finally, I could at least know if my body was able to recover and return to alignment again. Right before hearing my name being called by the nurse, I reached for my phone, lodged in the pocket of my purse, to look at a text message I had just received. To my surprise, it was 3:33 p.m.

Tears of joy ran down my cheeks. Once more, overloaded with gratitude, I gave thanks to the universe that was clearly nudging me many times to show that everything would be alright.

When the doctor entered the room, I was particularly happy to see him again. How lucky I was to have been under his care. The appointment was short and sweet. He explained the results from my scan, which sounded like a foreign language to us. But then, with enthusiasm, he confirmed some very good news. "Tanya, you are cancer FREE." In a split second, my life was changed, but this time for the better. With elation and infinite gratitude, I thanked him from the bottom of my heart for everything he did for me. He had been such a huge part of my journey, and I wanted him to know how blessed I was to have been touched by an angel who helped me get better and become myself again.

A second before parting our ways, we started walking in the corridor, and tears started flowing down my cheeks. Not tears of desperation, sadness, and fear, but tears of pure joy, relief, and bliss. I could finally go home, take some time to recover from all the stress my mind, body, and soul had gone through, and with time, begin looking at the future with hope and excitement.

It is now 9:14 p.m., and I am profoundly tired but so thankful for what life with cancer has taught me along the way. I know I have months of recuperation ahead of me, but I can't help but feel appreciative of how enlightening this experience has been. It has made me a stronger and more resilient human being. The biggest lesson I am taking away from all of this is that I am the most important person in my life. By taking care of myself and filling my own energy reserve as much as I can, I know I will always be in a better position to help others in their own unique and transformative healing journey, as well.

I hope that my story will inspire you
to take care of yourself,
to trust your intuition,
to advocate for yourself,

to speak your authentic voice,
to love yourself unconditionally and
trust that there is a higher power
always close to cheer you up
and support you anytime you are in need.

I wish you love, healing, and wholeness.

Tanya xx

Butterfly Tattoo

Eight years ago, my uncle André, my father's brother lost his wife to cancer. To somehow be able to cope with his grief and ease the unbearable pain of losing her, he decided to get a gorgeous artwork of her portrait tattooed on his chest. As an artist, when he showed it to me, I was blown away by how beautiful and realistic it looked.

A couple of years later, I finally decided to have two artworks tattooed on my body by the same artist who created my uncle's wonderful tattoo.

The first one was a large rose, the highest vibrational flower on earth and a symbol of unconditional love. The second one was a beautiful feather on my left shoulder, reminding me of the eternal connection to my loved ones, God, and the angels in heaven.

I told my husband after my surgery that I wanted to get a butterfly tattoo on my left wrist as a symbol of healing and transformation when I would be feeling better and have more energy.

The same week I received the wonderful news that the cancer was no longer present within my physical body, I got a call from my mother letting me know that my uncle André, who was also battling kidney cancer, had entered the palliative care unit. The disease had spread in his entire body, and he now only had a few months or weeks ahead of him before leaving his physical body and returning back home.

His soul passed away on December 18. Even though I was feeling the sadness of losing him, I also felt relief and peace for his soul that was released from the immeasurable pain and discomfort he must have been dealing with in the past few months. A couple of days later, I heard that his celebration of life was scheduled on January 6, 2023.

During the holidays, just after a morning walk, I felt compelled to call the tattoo parlor to hopefully get an appointment soon. The lovely lady who answered browsed over their very busy schedule for a couple of minutes to see if she could fit me in the same week. After a couple of minutes, she came back on the phone and said that the only opening she would have for me would be on January 6, 2023, at three o'clock. I then went into my calendar and remembered that my uncle's celebration of life was on the same day.

At that moment, I knew it was my uncle who had orchestrated everything. This time, he wanted to let me know that he would be present with me in pure energy while I was getting my little butterfly tattooed on my arm. It was such a blessing to have this powerful sign from the universe, comforting me that he was now home and well. Even from above, he would be present with me while I was getting my new set of wings, transformed and healed.

We are always connected and at arm's reach. Our loved ones and our entire team of helpers in heaven are always only a thought away. I am so grateful that this new tattoo will be much more than a reminder of the major transformation my spiritual, mental, emotional, and physical bodies went through last year but will also be a symbol of the timeless and limitless connection I have with everyone and everything.

And again, like the cardinals who showed up for me at the beginning of my journey, this was truly a wonderful and powerful gift I received, starting a fresh new year where everything will be possible.

Thank You

To my husband Stéphane, my son Jacob, and my daughter Maïka. You all have been my inexhaustible source of strength, support, and comfort. This disease was hard on all of us. Even in the most difficult moments, it was important for me to laugh and spend quality time together. I know it was not only affecting me but was also hard for you as well in your own way. I've learned that each situation placed in front of us is always a lesson and opportunity to support and love each other more. I love you and will be there for all of you. Always.

To my mom and dad. Thank you for your support, unconditional love, home-cooked meals, gifts, and visits to the hospital where I was in my most vulnerable state. It has brought me so much comfort knowing you are here for me and you know, in return, I will always be there for both of you too. I love you from the bottom of my heart, and I am forever grateful that you have decided to be my parents.

To my sister Natalie. The universe has played its cards well, and we could finally connect again in a way that hasn't been possible in the past few years. I am grateful for this time to be there for each other and be honest with each other, finding peace and learning opportunities to heal and embody who we truly are as humans, daughters, sisters, and mothers. I love you, and I am grateful we have each other.

To all my wonderful and beloved friends, work colleagues, neighbors, and complete strangers I had the opportunity to talk with and who have listened, supported, and cheered me greatly throughout this life-changing event. I am deeply grateful for all your beautiful gestures that brought me hope in these very challenging times.

To Julie. I will be eternally grateful to have you in my life and have you as my dearest friend. We have developed such a strong and beautiful relationship throughout the years that is always flourishing and getting stronger. Thank you for being YOU, for sharing our tears, our many laughs, our deep conversations, and your comforting presence. You know I am always just a call away and that I will also be there for you too, no matter what.

To Tammy. I cannot express to you how much you have helped me find myself again. You are such a gifted energy healer and a wise teacher. I feel so blessed to have you in my life as your student and a dear friend. I remember the first day we met at a cafe and getting the chills all over my body in a way I've never felt before. At that moment, I knew it was the beginning of a wonderful healing journey together. You helped me so much, and please know I am also there for you if you need anything.

To Olga. I am so appreciative to have met you many years ago and for having the opportunity to be your student and learn so many life lessons from a very special and wise soul. Mindfulness is now part of my daily life, and even in times of turbulence, I know how to connect with this quiet place inside of me, bringing me back to wholeness and joy again. Thank you for putting me in contact with Maureen. She has also been such a huge help to bring my body back to health. I am forever grateful for you. To Maureen. You have been godsent, and I want you to know how your naturopathic practice helped me so much to go through cancer with hope, positivity, and all the necessary tools my body needed to realign with its natural state. I remember when you asked me at our first appointment what I would do next after finding health again. This specific question truly gave me hope, and I am so very excited for what will be coming next in my life. Everything is possible now, and I thank you deeply for this.

To Ashley. Thank you for your support and for inspiring me to use my art as my medicine. It was one of the most powerful tools I used inside my healing toolbox all along the way. It helped me create this book and discover my voice in a way I've never done before. Also, listening to your podcast every week helped me stay rooted to the Earth and deeply connected to the divine at the same time. You are a very special human being, and I am so grateful that you are in my life and immensely thankful for your kind and beautiful forward for this book.

To Laura. When I discovered the diagnosis, I felt inspired to connect with you so you could access my Akashic records. I knew it would bring me the messages I needed to work on myself and to help my body become whole again. You are a very talented Akashic records reader, and I will always cherish the time within the Pleiades, learning more about the history of my soul. Healing is a lifelong journey, and I know I have many important missions I still need to accomplish before leaving this earthly plane to return home.

To Joy. Listening to your story has truly encouraged me to not lose hope, and I am so privileged to be wearing one of your gorgeous and ethereal pieces of jewelry on my finger every day. It is my unique lucky charm, reminding me of my strength and courage in this period of my life. Thank you for showing up in my life exactly when I needed it.

To Marie-Pierre. Your inner strength, ambition, and light-hearted and positive outtake on life are some of many traits that drew me to become your student and work with you. How you have decided to turn your life over and what you have created for yourself and your family after your cancer remission has been such an important source of inspiration for me and encouraged me to do the same. I feel so privileged to have been your student and work as a dynamic duo with you, creating the *Oracle de la lumière* just when the world pandemic started. I am so grateful that many people around the world, when using our deck of cards, will be divinely guided with the essence of both of our energies. I am blessed to call you my friend.

To Chantal. Meeting you online just after receiving my diagnosis and bathing in your powerful, positive, and divine energy was such a blessing for me. Hearing about your own unique journey through cancer changed my outlook on the disease, and I chose to see it as an opportunity to practice self-care more radically and accept and surrender to whatever I was going through. You are a true force of nature. I can't wait to give you a big hug and say out loud together that we are cancer survivors and thrivers!

To Mylène. The beautiful and powerful healing session I had with you was so special and enlightening for me. You were able to connect with my soul and understand things that I already knew inside but became clearer to my conscious mind within minutes. You are such a talented and soulful healer, and everyone on your path is lucky to be within your beautiful energy. Thank you for this divine moment.

To Diana. Thank you for giving me one of the most important lessons I needed to hear through this whole experience—to live in the present moment, one day at a time, and focus only on what I can control. It truly helped me to cross over my fears and remain at peace.

To Sasha and Simone. Two wonderful long-distance Instagram friends and thyroid and scoliosis survivors. Thank you for your valuable time, answering all my questions, and encouraging me through this rocky journey. It made me feel a little less alone. Know that if you need anything, I will always be one click away.

To Maria, Kevin, and Kelsey. Listening to your podcast *Heal Squad by Maria Menounos* brought me so much peace and a sense of community while learning so much about my own inner healing powers. Thank you for dedicating your life to helping others to find the right tools to become whole again. We are all in this together, and this is why it is always better together. Thank you, thank you, thank you.

To Genevieve. I am in such awe of how the universe connects similar souls together in a lifetime. It started with my intuition guiding me to pick up your book *Solace* in a Chapters during lunchtime. Connecting with you afterwards through Instagram, discovering we had so much in common, and having the immense privilege of working together crafting and bringing *Solstice* to life and making it available to all the world—for this, I will always be grateful. Thank you so much for putting your beautiful energy in this book.

To Adrian. I am so grateful for you taking of your precious time, energy, and expertise, reading through my story from the first to the last word, and sparkling it with your magic. It is so perfect and it truly reflects deeply what my soul wanted to share with the world. I thank you from the bottom of my heart for everything, and I hope to work with you again in the near future on future projects.

To Julie from *Rose aux Joues*. After my cancer diagnosis last year, it has been such a transformative journey for me. Spiritually, emotionally, mentally, and oh so physically. Since my surgery last year, I feel like I am in a different body and am still figuring out how to adjust to it. It is definitely a process. Thank you from the bottom of my heart for photographing me as the new woman I've become. It was so much fun, liberating, and it helped me embrace my new scars and body, with all the challenges I've been experiencing in the last few years. I will be forever grateful for your talent, your profoundness, and your passion to share the story of many women as unique and perfect as they are. You truly are the angel of Kodak.

To God, the angels, my ancestors, and my guides. Even if you are invisible to my eyes, I know and have faith that you are surrounding me with all your love, comfort, and healing vibrations. Thank you for listening to my prayers and intentions and for being with me every step of the way.

And finally, a huge thanks to YOU, my beautiful reader, who took some of your precious time to read my story and be inspired by poetry that brought me so much hope and comfort through the last year. I never felt alone—not even for one instant—while writing this book. I felt supported and embraced by an infinite amount of love and comfort, and I hope this book will give you the strength, support, and introspection you need for yourself in your own healing journey. Know you are always supported and loved.

I am now transformed, with a new set of wings. Free of the past, grateful for all the beauty within the present, and hopeful for a better future for myself and the generations to come.

The Author

Tanya is an artist, writer, energy healer, quiet leader, mother, daughter, wife, and cancer survivor. She lives in Ottawa, Canada, with her soulmate and her two children.

tanyamontpetit.com
instagram.com/tanya.montpetit
facebook.com/tanya.c.montpetit

A portion of the profits from each book sale will be donated to the Canadian Cancer Society, dedicated to improving the lives of people affected by cancer for over 80 years. Support cancer research and help people live longer, fuller lives.

Thank you from the bottom of my heart.

For More Information on Thyroid Cancer:

https://cancer.ca/en/cancer-information/cancer-types/thyroid

https://www.thycansurvivors.org

https://www.thyroidcancercanada.org

Solstice © 2023
Copyright by Tanya Montpetit

Photography | Julie Dessureault
Cover and interior design | Tanya Montpetit
Copyediting | Genevieve G. Georget
Proofreading | Adrian Bumgarner

All rights reserved. No part of this publication may be reproduced, stored in a retrieval system or transmitted in any form or by any means – electronic, mechanical, photocopying, and recording or otherwise – without prior written permission from the author.

First edition: June 2023
ISBN: 9781738015207

www.ingramcontent.com/pod-product-compliance
Lightning Source LLC
Chambersburg PA
CBHW071334080526
44587CB00017B/2829